Let's Light Up the Sky

A Musical Play for Christmas

Dawn Elizabeth Harris

RELIGIOUS AND MORAL EDUCATION PRESS

Religious and Moral Education Press
A division of SCM-Canterbury Press Ltd
A wholly owned subsidiary of Hymns Ancient & Modern Ltd
St Mary's Works, St Mary's Plain
Norwich, Norfolk NR3 3BH

Copyright © 2000 Dawn Elizabeth Harris

Dawn Elizabeth Harris has asserted her right under the Copyright, Designs and Patents Act, 1988, to be identified as Author of this Work.

All rights reserved. Parts of this book may be photocopied by the purchaser or the purchaser's school/organization for use within that school/organization only. The photocopying of inspection copies is not permitted.

First published 2000

ISBN 1 85175 252 8

Dedicated to Joseph Oliver,
my precious son.

Audiocassette

A *Let's Light Up the Sky* audiocassette (ISBN 1 85175 253 6) may be ordered from RMEP at the address above, or telephone 01603 612914.
This cassette includes backing-tracks for all the songs, which many schools will find invaluable for rehearsals. Please note that the cassette is *not available on inspection*.

Design, illustration and typesetting by
Martin Harris Creative Media, Torquay
www.mhcreativemedia.com

Printed in Great Britain by
David Gregson Associates,
Beccles, Suffolk
for SCM-Canterbury Press Ltd, Norwich

CONTENTS

Characters
4

Introduction
5

The Songs
5

Stage Set, Props
and Costumes
7

The Play
11

The Music
27

Form for registration
of amateur performing rights
47

Let's Light Up the Sky

CHARACTERS

Christmas Star: Sings a solo and has a fairly large speaking part. The children might like to choose an appropriate name for this character.

Angel 1 (Angie): Sings a solo and has a fairly large speaking part. If a boy is cast as this character then an alternative name to 'Angie' will be needed. This could be chosen by the children.

Stars 1, 2 and 3: Small speaking parts.

Mary: Small speaking part with an optional solo to sing.

Joseph: Small speaking part with an optional solo to sing.

Roman Soldier: Small speaking part.

Innkeepers 1, 2 and 3: Non-speaking parts.

Innkeeper 4: Small speaking part.

Shepherds 1, 2 and 3: Sing a song together and have small speaking parts.

Angels 2, 3 and 4: Sing a song with the Choir and have small speaking parts.

Wise Men 1, 2 and 3: Sing a song together and have small speaking parts.

NON-SPEAKING GROUPS

Crowd: For a short scene in Nazareth.

The script also offers various opportunities to bring additional **Angels** or **Stars** on stage in non-speaking roles or as dancers, if desired.

INTRODUCTION

This musical play for Christmas has been specially written for primary children and can be adapted in various ways to suit the needs of individual schools. The play script is short and simple, and most speaking parts could be easily learnt by younger pupils. If you are planning a mixed-age production, older pupils could take the two main parts, with the younger children in the Choir or playing the other characters.

SPECIAL NEEDS

As a Special Needs teacher, I am keen, as with my other books, to see this play enjoyed by S.E.N. children. The songs, particularly, are easy to learn, with tunes that are picked up quickly and lend themselves to rhythmic accompaniment and simple dance work.

In our (special) school, we give children the opportunity to say their lines as well as they can, with an adult narrator filling in the narrative as necessary to make it clear to the audience what is happening.

THE SONGS

The singers are central to the success of the play as the songs carry the action along. The Choir could wear a simple uniform costume to match the theme of the play - for example, a sweatshirt with a star pinned on the front and/or a simple star headband. If some of the Choir are also your dancers, they can then move onto the stage quickly and easily, already in costume.

SOLOS

There are several solo parts in the songs, but if you do not have confident soloists, the solo sections can be identified by dividing the Choir into small groups to sing the different parts.

DO WE NEED A BAND?

Several songs lend themselves to rhythmic accompaniment and this can be produced by a separate 'band' using school percussion instruments. However, as some songs do not require percussion, a few Choir members could have responsibility for playing in the songs that do, if a separate band stretches your numbers.

DO WE NEED A PIANIST?

If you listen to the accompanying *Let's Light Up the Sky* audiocassette (see page 2), you will hear that I use a strong rhythm on the keyboard to hold the songs together. I find that children sing so much better when they can feel a strong pulse. If a pianist or keyboard player is not available, your children could sing along to the backing-tracks provided on the audiocassette. I have seen this strategy work very well.

The score has deliberately been kept very simple, so that pianists or keyboard players are not daunted by lots of black notes while the class runs riot! More adventurous pianists will be able to embellish the accompaniment if they wish.

Guitar chords are also included for teachers who prefer this instrument.

STAGE SET, PROPS AND COSTUMES

The play requires a distinction to be made between action taking place in 'Heaven', involving angels and stars, and action taking place on 'Earth', involving the human Nativity characters. Overleaf is a stage plan suitable if your hall allows a two-tier arrangement. The height difference need not be great, depending on how many stage blocks are available and how safe you feel such a set would be for your pupils.

IN HEAVEN

A back-drop of a star-filled sky would be adequate for scenes in Heaven.

A focal point for conversation between Christmas Star and Angel 1 is a mirror where they make themselves look good, ready to appear in the sky. A swivel mirror would be fine, but a foil one with cardboard surround could be constructed as an ICT project if glass is considered inadvisable on stage.

A simple rail could be placed around the edge of Heaven so that children don't fall off.

ON EARTH

A traditional Nativity scene is built up on Earth as a tableau as the play progresses. A simple bale of hay/straw is always successful as a seat for Mary and Joseph. A painted stable back-drop is desirable but not essential.

Mary enters first with a wicker basket full of clothes that she sorts and folds. Other props for human characters include:

- sign reading 'A few months later'
- scroll for Roman soldier
- inn signs
- brooms for innkeepers
- large bundles for Joseph to carry as baggage
- doll representing the baby Jesus and a manger (both to be brought out from behind the hay-bale at the point when Jesus is born)
- camp 'fire' as a focal point for the shepherds
- toy lamb
- telescopes for the wise men
- gifts of 'gold, frankincense and myrrh'

STAGE SET

Stage blocks arranged on two levels for Heaven and Earth with a step between the two.

Palm trees and clouds cut out of thin hardboard or mdf.

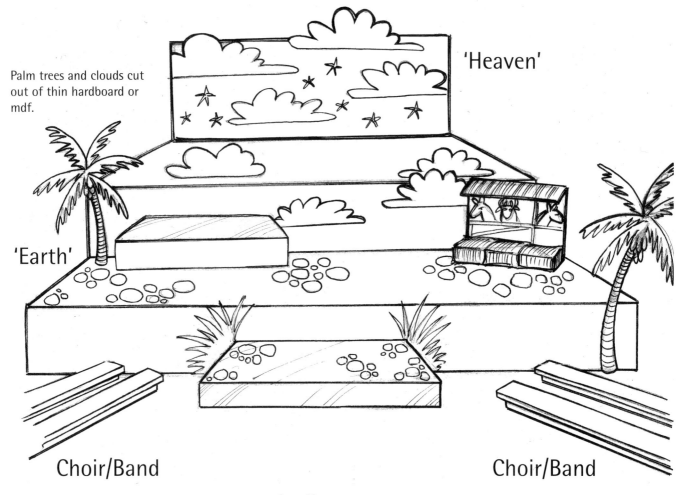

'Heaven'

'Earth'

Choir/Band   Choir/Band

Audience

PROPS

Heavenly mirror
Made from full-length mirror covered with a cloud-shaped frame jig-sawed from thin mdf or hardboard.

Free-standing clouds
Cloud shapes cut out of mdf and secured with two fixed stands.

Let's Light Up the Sky

Stable background
Animals in stalls painted on board. Lightweight roof made from strong card covered with strips of straw to look like thatch. Brackets secured behind and weighted down. Real bales of hay at front of backdrop.

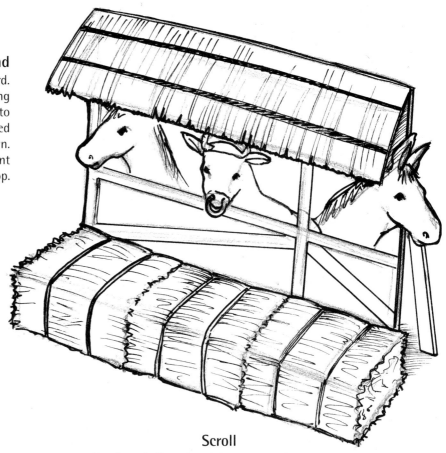

Free-standing hotel signs
Hotel signs created as cut-out on one piece of light mdf painted and bracketed behind to enable signs to stand freely.

Scroll
Scroll made from two tubes saved from aluminium foil packaging. Push plasticine down each hole to secure short off-cuts of dowling. Manuscript made from unused newsprint.

Shepherds' fire
Build basic fire from tubes saved from aluminium foil packaging. Stick tubes to circular piece of card. Paint brown and black. Create flames from red and orange tissue paper.

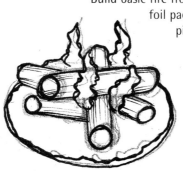

COSTUMES

Dancers' ribbons
Some of the songs provide opportunities for dance by children in simple star or angel costumes. Ribbons are very successful tools for dancers and can be easily waved around if attached to a hair 'scrunchie' slipped onto the wrist.

Angels' wings
Card angel wings with halo attached and strings that thread through gown to keep them in position.

An alternative is to use old net curtains attached to back and wrists.

Simple tunic
Fold large sheet to a square. Cut hole round plate for head. Sew up two sides leaving armholes. Dye sheet black, draw large star and spray with silver paint.

Simple star headbands
Cover strip of card with tin foil. Staple two ends together the correct shape for the child's head and then stick on a cut-out star, again covered with tin foil. Decorate with glitter, silver spray or tinsel.

The dancers could wear one of these headbands each. Also a black sweatshirt with pinned silver stars.

Let's Light Up the Sky

The Play

Note Throughout the play, the stage area representing Heaven is referred to as the 'upper stage' and the area representing Earth as the 'lower stage' (see sketch of two-tier set on page 8). The action moves from one stage area to the other only where indicated in the stage directions.

(Christmas Star enters and stands upper stage left in front of the mirror, preening him/herself. Hanging by the mirror is an outer coat for Angel 1 and a star headband. Christmas Star puts on the headband, turns about to see his/her back and admires him/herself in the mirror. Looks pleased. Enter Angel 1 stage left.)

Angel 1: Ooh, very good, Superstar *(or use name)*. You look great!

Christmas Star *(still looking in the mirror)*: Not bad, eh? *(Turns to face Angel 1.)* So, what brings you here?

Angel 1: It's happened again!

Christmas Star: What has?

Angel 1: Gabriel's had another special job to do today. Why **him** again?

Christmas Star: I don't know, Angie *(or use alternative name)*. What has he had to do this time?

Angel 1: He had to sort out a chap called Joseph. He'd got upset and confused about his wife having a baby, or something. Gabriel didn't tell me the details.

Christmas Star: It was only a little while ago that Gabriel went to tell a lady about having a baby, wasn't it?

Angel 1: Yes, you're right. *(Pauses to think.)* I wonder if the two are connected?

Let's Light Up the Sky

Christmas Star: I expect they are! Still, don't look so fed up, Angie *(or use alternative name)*. I'm sure you will be given a task some day soon.

Angel 1: But **when**?

Christmas Star: I don't know, but I've heard that one of us in here in Heaven is going to be telling people on Earth about the birth of a special king!

Angel 1: Just one of us? Most likely you!
(Pauses and has a long look at her/himself in the mirror.)
But I do have more shiny bits. *(Touches halo and wings proudly.)*
You're not **all** that bright, are you?

Christmas Star: You've no idea how bright I can be once I get up in the sky. I'd just like the chance.

(Enter Stars 1, 2 and 3, running on excitedly from a 'job'.)

Star 1: What a beautiful display we made tonight!

Star 2: I think we took the prize tonight, guys.

Star 3: We're a good team, us lot!

(Stars 1, 2 and 3 slap each other's hands in 'give me five' fashion.)

Star 1 *(looking at Christmas Star)*: Why are you looking so fed up?

Star 2: Still not picked for a job?

Star 3: Still hoping you'll be chosen for the **big** shine, are you?

(Stars 1, 2 and 3 laugh together.)

Christmas Star: Well, someone's going to be, and I **am** rather large and bright!

Star 1: We'll just have to wait and see.

Star 2: Come on, guys, I'm exhausted. Let's go and get some rest.

(All Stars except Christmas Star exit.)

SONG 1: ONE DAY WE'LL BE CHOSEN

(Sung by Christmas Star and Angel 1.)

Christmas Star:
1. In the wider scheme of things,
It's not such a big deal
When your dreams are dashed
And you face what is real.
Not everyone is chosen
To be in the limelight
But how I wish I could shine tonight.

Angel 1:
2. In the wider scheme of things,
It's not really a shame
When others have a task
Yet no one calls your name.
Not everyone is chosen
To be in the limelight
But how I wish I could sing tonight.

Christmas Star and Angel 1:
3. One day we'll be chosen,
One day we'll get the call,
One day, when we least expect,
We'll be there with them all.
Not everyone is chosen
To be in the limelight
But how we wish we could be there tonight.

(Exit Christmas Star and Angel 1. During the last part of the song, Mary enters on the lower stage. She is carrying a wicker basket of clothes. She puts down the basket, kneels beside it and starts folding the clothes. Enter Joseph. He walks towards Mary.)

Joseph: Hello, Mary.

(Mary smiles tentatively at him.)

Joseph *(putting an arm around her shoulders)*: Mary, I couldn't take in all that about the Angel coming to see you. Please tell me again what he said.

Mary: He said that I would become pregnant and my baby would be God's son!

Let's Light Up the Sky

Joseph: Well, an angel came to see me too. *(Mary stands up looking inquisitive.)* He told me the same. He said that everything will be fine.

(Mary and Joseph hug briefly. Mary picks up her basket and they exit.)

(Enter on lower stage Roman Soldier, Crowd, Mary and Joseph. One of the Crowd holds up a sign reading 'A few months later'. The Crowd whisper together and point at the Soldier as they wonder what he is going to say. The Soldier opens a scroll and addresses the Crowd. They stand very still, facing him.)

Soldier: It is a decree of Caesar Augustus that each man must return to his birthplace to be registered for a new tax. *(Exit.)*

(The Crowd turn in groups to discuss this news as they exit.)

Mary: Oh Joseph, it's going to be such a long and difficult journey.

Joseph: Yes, I wish my home town was nearer. Bethlehem is over a hundred miles from here.

Mary: I don't think I can walk all that way. Can you get a donkey for me to ride?

Joseph: I'm sure I can. I'll look after you. Try not to worry, Mary.

(Mary and Joseph exit slowly, Joseph showing that he is looking after Mary, perhaps putting an arm around her or through hers.)

(Enter Innkeepers 1, 2, 3 and 4. To show the audience that the lower stage is now in Bethlehem, they put up, or hold up, signs showing the names of their inns, e.g. 'Bethlehem Hotel', 'Traveller's Rest', 'Tax-Payer's Inn'.

They then busy themselves with jobs such as sweeping the floor, wiping glasses, etc., as the music to the next song begins. Mary and Joseph meanwhile enter and walk around the hall, stopping in front of Innkeeper 1 at the beginning of Verse 1.

They then move on in time to stand still at the second inn and third inn to sing Verses 2 and 3. During the choruses, Innkeepers 1, 2 and 3 shake their heads and shrug their shoulders, indicating that they have no vacancies. There is scope here for children to add their own miming ideas.)

SONG 2: NO ROOM

(Sung by **Mary**, **Joseph** *and the* **Choir**.*)*

Choir:
1. Lonely and weary
They set off to Bethlehem.
Such a long journey
But there is no room for them.

CHORUS
No room, not even for a baby,
No room, not even for a king,
No room, not even for God's only son,
I'm sorry, you can't come in.

Mary:
2. Restless and tired,
My babe is soon to be born.
Please can you help us?
Oh please can we have a room?

CHORUS

Joseph:
3. Anxious and waiting,
My wife needs a place very soon.
Please can you help us?
Oh please can we have a room?

CHORUS

(As the song ends, **Innkeepers 1, 2** *and* **3** *exit.* **Mary** *and* **Joseph** *approach* **Innkeeper 4**.*)*

Innkeeper 4: Did you say the baby is due any time?

Joseph: Yes, my wife really needs to rest soon.

Innkeeper 4: I don't have any rooms, we're full to overflowing. But look *(pausing to think)* if you're absolutely desperate – how about using my stable?

Joseph: That's very kind, thank you.

Innkeeper 4: I'll clean it up a bit and give you some fresh straw. Come this way.

(Innkeeper 4 leads Mary and Joseph to the stable area, lower stage right.)

Innkeeper 4: I hope you'll be comfortable. Goodnight! *(Exit.)*

(Mary and Joseph settle down. During the next song, Mary can quietly pick up the 'baby Jesus' at the point when the song says that he was born.)

SONG 3: IN THE HUSH OF THE NIGHT

(Sung by the Choir.)

In the hush of the night
When Bethlehem was so still and quiet,
A couple knocked at the innkeeper's door
Only to hear the news, 'We can't take more.'

In the hush of the night
The stars above the inn were clear and bright.
The keeper found a place where animals lay,
This was the only place where they could stay.

And it was in the hush of the night
That a king was born for you and me,
And it was in the hush of the night
That angels sang for all to see.
Animals surrounded him,
Shepherds came to worship him,
Came to worship,
In the hush of the night.

(During the song, Christmas Star creeps onto the upper stage and settles down to sleep. When the song ends, Angel 1 rushes on.)

Angel 1: Hey, bright friend, guess what? I'm on now, centre sky! There's going to be a whole host of us but I've got the speaking part!

Christmas Star *(sleepily)*: What?

Angel 1: God's just told us. His son Jesus has been born – on Earth!
It's the biggest news ever! This is the special job I've been waiting for.

Christmas Star: Excellent! What have you got to do?

Angel 1: Just watch that sky and you'll find out.

(*Angel 1 rushes off, grabbing his/her 'outer coat'.*)

Christmas Star (*musing aloud*): Well, it looks like I didn't get picked for the job. Angie (*or use alternative name*) will be great though.

(*Shepherds enter lower stage left, carrying their 'fire' and a 'lamb'. They warm themselves by the fire, guarding their sheep. One or two Stars enter on the upper stage and stand very still, leaving space for Angels to pass in front. Christmas Star continues sleeping.*)

Shepherd 1: What a lovely clear night.

Shepherd 2 (*looking skywards*): Yes, the stars are beautiful. It's so still.

Shepherd 3 (*after a pause*): Still?? Still no longer! What on earth is **that**?

(*Enter Angels. Exit all Stars behind them.*)

SONG 4: AT LAST THE TIME HAS COME

(*Sung by the Angels and the Choir.*)

CHORUS
At last!
The time has come
To proclaim God's holy birth,
To bring God's peace on Earth -
A message for everyone.
Hallelujah!
At last!
The time has come
To proclaim God's holy birth,
To bring God's peace on Earth -
A message for everyone.

1. And so at last
Angels fill the sky
Shout it out on high -
The Lord has come!
Jesus is born!
At last, at last, at last the time has come!

CHORUS

Let's Light Up the Sky

2. And so at last
Let the angels sing,
The Christmas message bring -
A king for all,
Born in a stall!
At last, at last, at last the time has come!

CHORUS

3. And so at last
Kings and shepherds come.
This king's for everyone!
Bow to him,
He's the king.
At last, at last, at last the time has come!

CHORUS

Angel 1: Wonderful news! A special baby has been born tonight - a saviour for everyone!

Angel 2: Go to Bethlehem to see this baby!

Angel 3: You will find him in a stable.

Angel 4: Lying in a manger.

(Angels exit.)

Shepherd 1: Wow! What a sight!

Shepherd 2: Well, what do you think? Shall we go and see this saviour?

Shepherd 3: I'm not so sure. It's a long way down to Bethlehem.

Shepherd 1: Yes, and a long way to walk back up again!

SONG 5: IT'S A LONG WAY DOWN TO BETHLEHEM!

*(Sung by the **Shepherds**. The audience could be encouraged to join in and sing 'It's a long way down to Bethlehem' in Verses 2 and 3.)*

VERSE 1
Shepherd 1: Shall we go?
Shepherd 2: No! No! Shall we stay just so?
All: It's a long way down to Bethlehem!
Shepherd 1: Shall we do as they say?
Shepherd 2: Find a babe in the hay?
All: It's a long way down to Bethlehem!

VERSE 2
Shepherd 1: Shall we go to the inn?
Shepherd 2: What if nobody's in?
All: It's a long way down to Bethlehem!
Shepherd 1: Shall we take him a lamb?
Shepherd 2: What, a ewe or a ram?
All: It's a long way down to Bethlehem!

VERSE 3
Shepherd 1: Shall we gather the sheep?
Shepherd 2: Shall we go back to sleep?
All: It's a long way down to Bethlehem!
Shepherd 1: Shall we run all the way?
Shepherd 2: No, I'd much rather stay.
All: It's a long way down to Bethlehem!

*(The **Shepherds** look at each other.)*

Shepherds *(together)*: Let's go! *(Exit, running.)*

*(Enter **Angels** on upper stage.)*

Angel 1: How fantastic! We made such a wonderful display. Those shepherds were amazed.

Angel 2: God always said there was an extra special job waiting.

Angel 3: It was worth the wait.

Angel 4: What a celebration. God's son's birthday!

Let's Light Up the Sky

Angel 1: I could sing all night! *(Sings.)* At last ...

Angel 3 *(interrupting)*: Yes, I'm sure you could, but we must rest.
   (Tries to drag **Angel 1** *towards exit.)*

Angel 1: Let go. I'm staying here to watch the shepherds as they find the baby.

*(***Angel 1*** sits down at the front of the upper stage, looking down on Earth. Other* **Angels** *exit.)*

(Enter **Shepherds** *lower stage left, looking for the stable. They approach the stable tentatively and speak to* **Joseph,** *who moves nearer as he sees them approaching.)*

Shepherd 1: We've come to see the new baby king.

Shepherd 2: This can't be the right place, surely?

Shepherd 3: You're not all sleeping in this stable, are you?

SONG 6: SIMPLY A BABY

(Sung by the **Choir.***)*

1. Simply a stable,
Simply a manger,
Simply a baby,
Just like any other.

CHORUS
But this is Jesus,
God's only son.
He's not simply a baby,
He's a king.

2. Simply a mother,
Simply a father.
Simply a baby,
Just like any other.

CHORUS

(The **Shepherds** *enter the stable and kneel down, offering a gift of a lamb. They then step aside and sit down.* **Joseph** *moves into the stable and sits beside* **Mary.***)*

*(Enter **Stars** on upper stage, chatting. **Angel 1** is still there sitting looking down on Earth.)*

Star 1: Where's Angie *(or use alternative name)*?

Star 2: I don't know.

Angel 1 *(shouting)*: I'm over here!

Christmas Star: Angie *(or use alternative name)*! How did it go?

Angel 1: Well, it was just amazing...

Christmas Star *(interrupting)*: It's **my** turn now! You'll never guess what -
   I'm going to lead the way for some important wise men to find a route to Bethlehem.

Angel 1: On your own?

Christmas Star *(proudly)*: Yep! That's why I'm so unusual - so they will notice me.

Angel 1: Excellent! What a time this has been! I'm watching you, Superstar.

*(**Angel 1** settles down again, upper stage left. **Christmas Star** moves to the centre of the upper stage and stands very still.*

*Other **Stars** stand upper stage right, very still.*

*The **Wise Men** enter lower stage left. They look through telescopes towards the sky but well away from **Christmas Star** initially. The gifts of gold, frankincense and myrrh should also be on the lower stage ready for the **Wise Men** to pick up after the next song.)*

Wise Man 1: I used to like this occupation, but maybe I'm getting too old now.
   Nothing seems to change much in these planets. *(Puts down his telescope.)*

Wise Man 2: Night after night we look at that sky and we see the same old stars.

Wise Man 3 *(looking towards **Christmas Star**)*: Now hold on, gentlemen, that's where you
   are wrong! Look right over there.

Wise Man 1 *(picking up his telescope again)*: **Wow**! Now that **is** a star!

*(During the next song the **Wise Men** keep looking towards **Christmas Star**, who could ad lib some small movements. Other **Stars** could also make constellation patterns.)*

SONG 7: STARS, STARS

(Sung by the Wise Men.)

CHORUS
Stars, stars, look at the stars.
We've studied them, we've watched them,
Compared them to Mars.
We know every planet formation,
We know every star constellation,
But what have we here?
This star did appear
And shone over all of our nation!
This star has something to say!

VERSE 1

Wise Man 1:	My friends, it seems very unlikely
	That this star should just choose to shine brightly.
Wise Man 2:	It's much larger, much larger by far
	And much brighter than any other star.
Wise Man 3:	It tells of a birth,
	A king born on Earth.
All:	This star has something to say!

CHORUS

VERSE 2

Wise Man 1:	This star is moving much nearer
	And its message is clearer and clearer.
Wise Man 2:	It surely has something to say.
	We must watch it come what may.
Wise Man 3:	It tells of a birth,
	A king born on Earth.
All:	This star has something to say!

CHORUS

VERSE 3

Wise Man 1:	My friends, can we make this assumption
	That this star has a heavenly function?
Wise Man 2:	Let us hurry and get on our way.
	We must travel all night and day.
Wise Man 3:	We'll go to the birth
	Of a king born on Earth.
All:	This star has something to say!

CHORUS

Wise Man 2: I'm sure this star pattern means a new king has been born.

Wise Man 3: Come, let us see where it leads.

Wise Man 1: Let's take these gifts with us.

(*The* **Wise Men** *pick up their gifts and turn towards* **Christmas Star** *but remain still for Verse 1 of the next song. Other* **Stars** *exit. During Verse 2,* **Christmas Star** *can come down from the upper stage and move through the hall, leading the* **Wise Men** *to the stable in the traditional manner. This involves some poetic licence in terms of the distinction between Heaven and Earth but allows more freedom of movement, since* **Angel 1** *is still seated on the upper stage. The song can be repeated as necessary to accommodate this 'journey'. If* **Christmas Star** *has difficulty singing and walking simultaneously, he/she could sing the whole song before setting off and move to an instrumental playing of the music. Alternatively, the song could be sung by the* **Choir**.*)*

SONG 8: ALL THE WAY TO BETHLEHEM

(Sung by **Christmas Star**.*)*

1. Shining, I am shining,
Shining so brightly.
Shining for all to see,
I am shining.
(Sung twice.)

Let's Light Up the Sky

2. All the way to Bethlehem,
All the way I'll lead them.
All the way to Bethlehem,
I am shining.

Shining, shining *(last time only)*.

(Christmas Star stands still at the back of the stable. The Wise Men present their gifts - they could say the names 'Gold', 'Frankincense', 'Myrrh' as they do so. The Wise Men then kneel to the side of the stable scene.)

(Angel 1 stands up, on the upper stage, looking down at Christmas Star.)

Angel 1 *(in a stage whisper):* Psst, Superstar *(or use name)*. You were great!

(Angel 1 winks at Christmas Star, then turns to address the audience.)

Angel 1: Wow! What a time this has been. It seems strange that Superstar *(or use name)* has ended up over a stable, though. It's not how **we** would have planned it at all!

(Enter all other Angels on upper stage.)

Angel 2: Hi, Angie *(or use alternative name)*. I think we may be needed over there. *(Points to the stable scene.)*

Angel 3: Yes, we're needed to do a bit of guardian-angel protection.

Angel 4: What a picture! God's son on Earth!

Angel 1 *(excitedly)*: What are we waiting for then? Let's go!

(All the Angels move down to the stable, on the lower stage. Angel 1 stands by Mary and Joseph and the other Angels at the back of the scene.)

(Enter other Stars on upper stage.)

Star 1: Well, Superstar *(or use name)* had a grand task in the end, didn't he/she?

Star 2: Yes, guiding the wise men all that way. What a task to wait for!

Star 3: I think we should all celebrate this birthday now and make the best display we possibly can!

All Stars *(together):* Yes, let's!

(Angels with ribbons and star dancers could all join on stage for a last happy dance to the final song.)

SONG 9: LET US LIGHT UP THE SKY

(Sung by All.)

1. Let us light up the sky tonight,
Make the whole sky fill with light.
Oh what a wonderful, wonderful sight –
It's Jesus's birthday!

2. Let us all join together and sing,
Let the chimes and church bells ring.
Oh, it's the birth of a baby king –
It's Jesus's birthday!

3. Let us all give a special loud cheer,
Let us shout for everyone to hear.
Oh, a special day is here -
It's Jesus's birthday!

THE END

The Music

SONG 1: ONE DAY WE'LL BE CHOSEN

*(Sung by **Christmas Star** and **Angel 1**.)*

cue ⸺

Star 2: Come on, guys, I'm exhausted. Let's go and get some rest.

*(All **Stars** except **Christmas Star** exit.)*

With feeling, sweetly   Words and music © 2000 Dawn Elizabeth Harris

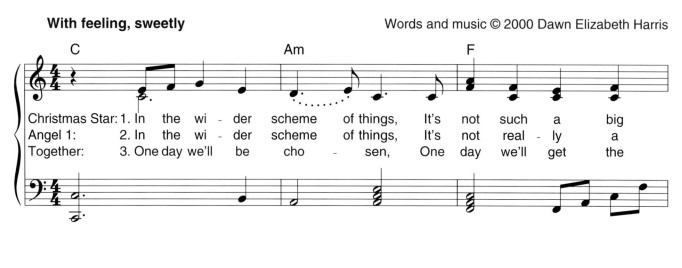

Christmas Star: 1. In the wi-der scheme of things, It's not such a big
Angel 1: 2. In the wi-der scheme of things, It's not real-ly a
Together: 3. One day we'll be cho-sen, One day we'll get the

deal   When your dreams are dashed And you face what is
shame   When oth-ers have a task Yet __ no one calls your
call,   One day, when we least ex - pect, We'll be there with them

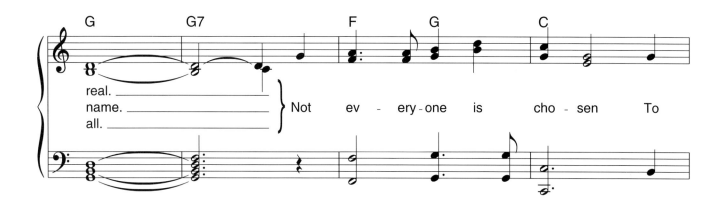

real. ⸺
name. ⸺   } Not ev-ery-one is cho-sen To
all. ⸺

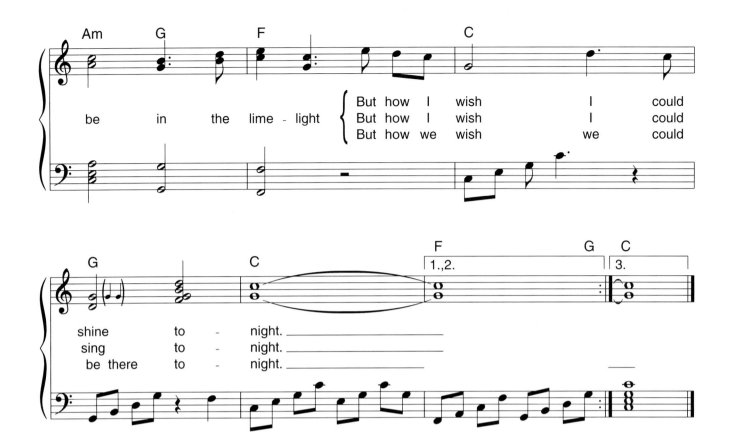

SONG 2: NO ROOM

*(Sung by **Mary, Joseph** and the **Choir**.)*

cue ────

*(Enter **Innkeepers** 1, 2, 3 and 4. They busy themselves with jobs such as sweeping the floor, wiping glasses, etc., as the music to the next song begins.)*

Notes on performing

As the music begins, Mary and Joseph enter and walk around the hall, stopping in front of Innkeeper 1 at the beginning of Verse 1. They then move on in time to stand still at the second inn and third inn to sing Verses 2 and 3. During the choruses, Innkeepers 1, 2 and 3 shake their heads and shrug their shoulders, indicating that they have no vacancies. There is scope here for children to add their own miming ideas.

Verses 2 and 3 could be sung by the Choir instead of being performed as solos by Mary and Joseph.

SONG 3: IN THE HUSH OF THE NIGHT

*(Sung by the **Choir**.)*

cue ⸺

Innkeeper 4: I hope you'll be comfortable. Goodnight! *(Exit.)*

SONG 4: AT LAST THE TIME HAS COME

*(Sung by the **Angels** and the **Choir**.)*

cue ⎯⎯⎯

Shepherd 3 *(after a pause)*: Still?? Still no longer! What on earth is **that?**
*(Enter **Angels**.)*

Words and music © 2000 Dawn Elizabeth Harris

At last! The time has come To pro-claim God's ho-ly birth, To bring God's peace on Earth A mess-age for ev-ery-one. Hal-le-lu-jah! At last! The time has come To pro-claim God's ho-ly birth, To

See overleaf for notes on performing 'At Last the Time has Come'.

Notes on performing 'At Last the Time has Come'

A rhythmic accompaniment on maracas, bongos and blocks could be added:

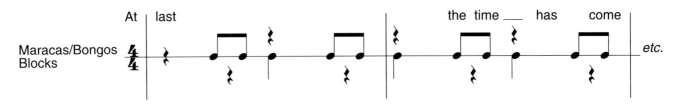

The Angels could perform a simple circle dance to a rhythmic accompaniment, using basic round-and-round and in-and-out routines. The Chorus could then be sung again.

SONG 5: IT'S A LONG WAY DOWN TO BETHLEHEM!

*(Sung by the **Shepherds**.)*

cue

Shepherd 3: I'm not so sure. It's a long way down to Bethlehem.
Shepherd 1: Yes, and a long way to walk back up again!

See overleaf for notes on performing *'It's a Long Way Down to Bethlehem!'*.

Notes on performing 'It's a Long Way Down to Bethlehem'

In this song, lines 1 and 4 of each verse are sung by Shepherd 1, lines 2 and 5 by Shepherd 2, and lines 3 and 6 by all the Shepherds, as shown below.

This song provides a good opportunity for audience participation, if so wished. One Shepherd could gesticulate to encourage everyone to sing 'It's a long way down to Bethlehem!' in Verses 2 and 3.

VERSE 1
Shepherd 1: Shall we go?
Shepherd 2: No! No! Shall we stay just so?
All: It's a long way down to Bethlehem!
Shepherd 1: Shall we do as they say?
Shepherd 2: Find a babe in the hay?
All: It's a long way down to Bethlehem!

VERSE 2
Shepherd 1: Shall we go to the inn?
Shepherd 2: What if nobody's in?
All: It's a long way down to Bethlehem!
Shepherd 1: Shall we take him a lamb?
Shepherd 2: What, a ewe or a ram?
All: It's a long way down to Bethlehem!

VERSE 3
Shepherd 1: Shall we gather the sheep?
Shepherd 2: Shall we go back to sleep?
All: It's a long way down to Bethlehem!
Shepherd 1: Shall we run all the way?
Shepherd 2: No, I'd much rather stay.
All: It's a long way down to Bethlehem!

SONG 6: SIMPLY A BABY

*(Sung by the **Choir**.)*

cue

Shepherd 2: This can't be the right place, surely?
Shepherd 3: You're not all sleeping in this stable, are you?

SONG 7: STARS, STARS

(Sung by the Wise Men.)

cue ⸻

Wise Man 1 *(picking up his telescope again)*: **Wow!** Now that **is** a star!

SONG 8: ALL THE WAY TO BETHLEHEM

(Sung by Christmas Star.)

cue ——————

Wise Man 2: I'm sure this star pattern means a new king has been born.
Wise Man 3: Come, let us see where it leads.
Wise Man 1: Let's take these gifts with us.

Words and music © 2000 Dawn Elizabeth Harris

1. Shi - ning, I am shi - ning. Shi - ning so

bright - ly. Shi - ning for all to see, I am

shi - ning. 2. All the way to Beth - le - hem,

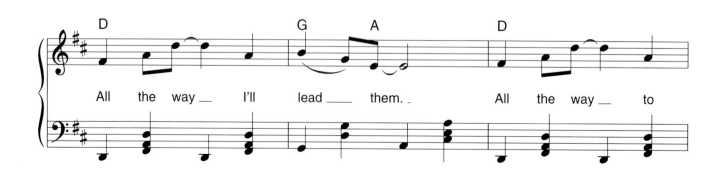

All the way I'll lead them. All the way to

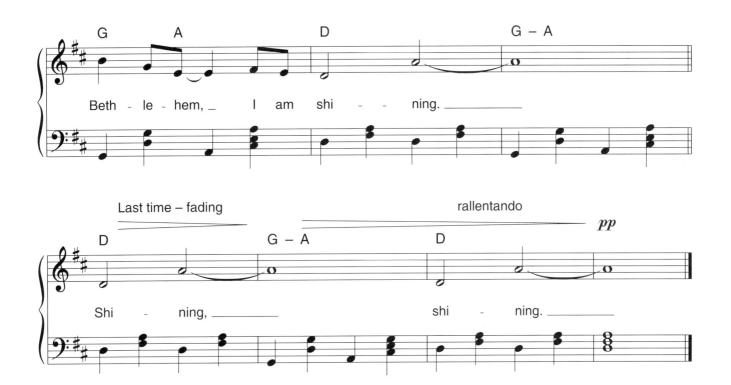

Notes on performing

The Wise Men pick up their gifts and turn towards Christmas Star but remain still for the Verse 1 of this song. During Verse 2, Christmas Star can come down from the upper stage and move through the hall, leading the Wise Men to the stable in the traditional manner. The song can be repeated as necessary to accommodate this 'journey'.

If Christmas Star has difficulty singing and walking simultaneously, he/she could sing the whole song before setting off and move to an instrumental playing of the music. Alternatively, the song could be sung by the Choir.

SONG 9: LET US LIGHT UP THE SKY

*(Sung by **All**.)*

cue ———

Star 3: I think we should all celebrate this birthday now and make the best display we possibly can!
All Stars *(together)*: Yes, let's!

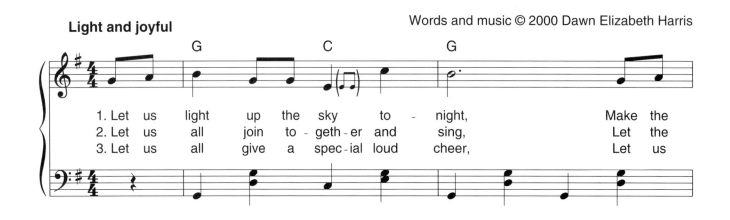

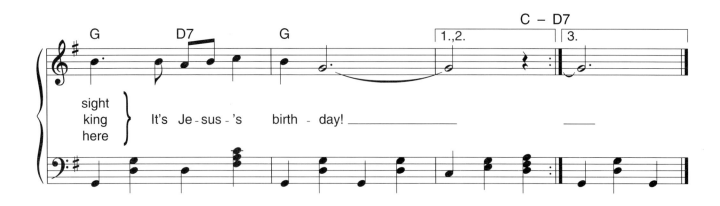

Notes on performing

This song can involve the whole cast as well as the Choir. The Stars could step forward to sing Verse 1 and the Angels to sing Verse 2, returning to their positions around the stable. The Choir could join the cast on stage for Verse 3. The whole song could be repeated with the audience encouraged to clap the rhythm below.
Also (second time through), extra words could be shouted or sung at the ends of lines 1 and 2 as follows:

VERSE 1
... tonight, *shine, shine, shine*, Make ...
... with light, *so bright*, Oh, ...

VERSE 2
... and sing, *la, la, la*, Let ...
... bells ring, *ding, dong*. Oh, ...

VERSE 3
... loud cheer, *hooray*, Let ...
... to hear, *hooray*. Oh, ...

Any percussion instruments can be used to accompany a strong keyboard rhythm, emphasizing the first and third beats:

IMPORTANT NOTE
PERFORMING RIGHTS FOR
LET'S LIGHT UP THE SKY

The purchaser of this book will normally be granted permission to perform LET'S LIGHT UP THE SKY in public free of charge for as many performances as required, subject to the following conditions:

1. The form below must be completed and a photocopy returned to the publishers three weeks in advance of the initial performance.

2. Permission is granted solely for amateur stage performances, and this permission does not confer the right to record the work visually or in sound.

3. Film recording and television rights are strictly reserved. Application for any of these must be made to the publishers, with this exception: an extract not exceeding two minutes in length may be taken from an amateur performance for broadcast on radio or television without reference to the publishers.

4. Performance by professional organizations is strictly forbidden without reference to the publishers.

Amateur Performing Rights Registration
LET'S LIGHT UP THE SKY

Purchaser's Name: ....

School, Church or Organization: ....

Address: ....

Details of initial performance(s): ....

Name and address of hall or auditorium at which performance(s) will take place:

....

Date(s) on which performance(s) will take place: ....

Total number of performances: ....

I understand that the completion and return of this form to RMEP, SCM-Canterbury Press Ltd, St Mary's Works, St Mary's Plain, Norwich, Norfolk NR3 3BH, automatically grants the school, church or organization named above permission to perform LET'S LIGHT UP THE SKY on the date(s) specified, and on any subsequent date(s) in the future. It is understood and agreed that this permission applies to the above organization or body only, and the book will be used solely by the original purchaser. Performances will be by amateurs and will not be made for commercial gain.

Signed (representative of purchasing organization): ....